O9-ABE-381

Rabbits on the Farm

by Mari C. Schuh

Consulting Editor: Gail Saunders-Smith, Ph.D.

Consultant: Cary J. Trexler, Ph.D., Assistant Professor
California Agricultural Experiment Station
University of California, Davis

Pebble Books

an imprint of Capstone Press
Mankato, Minnesota

j636.93
sch

MC

Pebble Books are published by Capstone Press
151 Good Counsel Drive, P.O. Box 669, Mankato, Minnesota 56002
http://www.capstone-press.com

© 2003 by Capstone Press. All rights reserved.
No part of this publication may be reproduced in whole or in part,
or stored in a retrieval system, or transmitted in any form or by any means,
electronic, mechanical, photocopying, recording, or otherwise,
without written permission of the publisher.
For information regarding permission, write to Capstone Press,
151 Good Counsel Drive, P.O. Box 669, Dept. R, Mankato, Minnesota 56002.
Printed in the United States of America.

1 2 3 4 5 6 08 07 06 05 04 03

Library of Congress Cataloging-in-Publication Data
Schuh, Mari C., 1975–
Rabbits on the farm / by Mari C. Schuh.
    p. cm.—(On the farm)
    Summary: Simple text and pictures introduce rabbits and their lives on a farm.
    Includes bibliographical references (p. 23) and index.
    ISBN 0-7368-1663-1 (hardcover)
    1. Rabbits—Juvenile literature. [1. Rabbits.] I. Title. II. Series: Schuh, Mari C.,
1975– . On the farm.
SF453.2 .S36 2003
636.9′322—dc21   2002008967

Note to Parents and Teachers

The On the Farm series supports national science standards related to life science. This book describes and illustrates rabbits and their lives on the farm. The photographs support early readers in understanding the text. The repetition of words and phrases helps early readers learn new words. This book also introduces early readers to subject-specific vocabulary words, which are defined in the Words to Know section. Early readers may need assistance to read some words and to use the Table of Contents, Words to Know, Read More, Internet Sites, and Index/Word List sections of the book.

Table of Contents

Some rabbits live on farms.
Some rabbits are tame.
Other rabbits are wild.

Most rabbits live in hutches.

buck

doe

A buck is a male rabbit.

A doe is a female rabbit.

A bunny is a young rabbit.

Rabbits need food, water, and bedding. They also need a hiding place in their hutches.

People feed hay and pellets to rabbits. People keep the hutches clean.

Some people keep rabbits
as pets. Some people
raise rabbits for their
meat and fur.

Other people breed and show rabbits. Some people who show rabbits win ribbons or prizes.

Rabbits use their
strong hind legs to hop.

Rabbits sniff.

Words to Know

breed—to raise animals in order to make more animals; many people who breed rabbits sell them to other people.

hind legs—the back legs of an animal

hutch—a small pen or coop where small animals live

pellets—small, hard pieces of food; pellets give rabbits the fiber and nutrients they need; rabbits can also eat a small amount of vegetables.

pet—a tame animal kept for company or pleasure; some wild rabbits live on farms, but they do not make good pets.

show—to take part in an exhibit or a contest

sniff—to breathe in quickly through the nose; rabbits have a very good sense of smell.

tame—trained to live with or be useful to people

wild—natural and not tamed by people

Read More

Frost, Helen. *Rabbits.* All About Pets. Mankato, Minn.: Pebble Books, 2001.

Klingel, Cynthia Fitterer, and Robert B. Noyed. *Rabbits.* Wonder Books. Chanhassen, Minn.: Child's World, 2001.

Sharth, Sharon. *Rabbits.* Nature Books. Chanhassen, Minn.: Child's World, 2000.

Internet Sites

Track down many sites about rabbits.
Visit the FACT HOUND at *http://www.facthound.com*

IT IS EASY! IT IS FUN!

1) Go to *http://www.facthound.com*

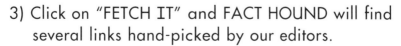

2) Type in: 0736816631

3) Click on "FETCH IT" and FACT HOUND will find several links hand-picked by our editors.

Relax and let our pal FACT HOUND do the research for you!

Index/Word List

Word Count: 103
Early-Intervention Level: 11

Credits
Heather Kindseth, series designer; Patrick D. Dentinger, book designer;
Deirdre Barton, photo researcher

Capstone Press/Gary Sundermeyer, cover, 8 (both); Nancy White, 1, 6, 10, 12, 16, 20
Index Stock Imagery/Myrleen Cate, 14
Lenz/Premium Stock/PictureQuest, 18
Unicorn Stock Photos/Gary Randall, 4

The author dedicates this book to Jason Rouvel and to her pet rabbit, Karma.